The Divine Keys

—∞—

Illuminating the Path to Oneness

Robin H. Clare

CreateSpace Publisher
ISBN: 1539105431
ISBN: 9781539105435
Library of Congress Control Number: 2016916980
CreateSpace Independent Publishing Platform
North Charleston, South Carolina

Interior Photography: Garrett Clare
Copyeditors: Lois Grasso, Ori Clare, Leslie Korus

On the Cover

The White Heron kept the author company at sunrise on Good Harbor Beach in Gloucester, Massachusetts. One of the locals said that a White Heron was a very rare sight in those parts. Nature is one of the many sources through which Divine wisdom is available to each and every one of us – and as a divinely guided person, Robin was curious to know what message the Heron had brought for her.

The Heron is a beautiful creature, exhibiting grace and noble stature. In Egypt, the Heron is honored as the creator of light. In China, the Heron represents strength, purity, patience and long life. In Africa, the Heron is thought to communicate with the Gods. Native Americans revere the Heron as a symbol of wisdom.

On that day, Robin resonated most with this message: *As a water creature, the Heron is a symbol of going with the flow, and working with the elements of Mother Nature, rather than struggling against Her.* Deeply drawn to the ocean and all of nature, Robin became even more inspired to complete this book, *The Divine Keys.*

More about the symbolism of the Heron can be found at:
www.symbolic-meanings.com.

Praise for The Divine Keys

"*The Divine Keys* is a precious treasure that holds a golden key to the peace, joy and love of our original creation. I believe the most powerful messages are those distilled into rich, filling nuggets of truth, and Robin has accomplished this with grace. Give yourself the gift of a lifetime and allow the wealth of wisdom in this extraordinary book to transform your world."
Jannirose Fenimore, Spiritual Author, Speaker and Teacher

"I love the interactive adventure that *The Divine Keys* provides. I love the pictures and self-examination questions. It is so much more than an intellectual experience, it is a wonderful opportunity for self-inquiry and reflection."
Edie Grossi, Reiki Master

"We (Angelic Council of LIGHT) love the book. You have taken accumulated wisdom of the worlds and put it into a form that is easy to read, understand and do. The great gift in this book is that anyone, at any level of spiritual learning, can achieve success with this book by following your easy directions."
Pat Caffrey, Angelic Council of LIGHT

"I do practice living a divinely guided life and Robin captured the key elements perfectly! Robin has been walking the walk for many years now and it's a joy to see her singing it from the rooftops. In this book, she has brought forth a powerful and shining example of how Divine Love graces her life and shows us how we can all live in the feeling of Oneness."
Maureen Ross Gemme, Emerge Leadership Academy LLC

"In *The Divine Keys*, Robin presents a beautiful and soulful, yet logical and simple path towards realizing our oneness with spirit, the wisdom of our hearts and our divine right to access the true potential of our spiritual journey."
Donna Rioux, Energy Medicine Practitioner

"Robin is a master at making dreams come true because she gives the world divine content which can be applied to many contexts. It doesn't have to be complicated to work through next steps. Robin has proven this over and over again. *The Divine Keys* can work for anyone, any time."
Dr. Alexandra Bakos, Mediator, Educational Consultant, Seimei teacher

"*The Divine Keys* is an easy 3-part practice into a deeply profound body of work. Robin does a beautiful job guiding you through what may be the greatest shift you'll ever make. From identifying your own personal relationship with Spirit to committing to your personal journey and, finally, integrating and living from your sacred self. This book will surely change your life as every magical image helps to activate each key within you."
Colleen Morgan, Metaphysical Teacher, The Spirit of Light

"This small gem of a contemplative book is your perfect take-along spiritual companion for the road warrior or parent-on-the run, whether an experienced seeker or newbie on the spiritual path. From the guiding white heron on its cover thru to its last pages of a receding sun, Robin gifts you with a smorgasbord of 18 contemplative keys of her divinely inspired teachings to keep you on your spiritual path anywhere, and everywhere."
Karen Sands, MCC, BCC, Best-Selling Author & Leading GeroFuturist℠

This book is dedicated to my father, Dr. George Handler,
for making his divine presence known and for sharing perfect guidance.

Introduction

"Come and teach with me where I AM," Yeshua beckoned me once again. I listened in awe as this highly-revered Ascended Master (most often referred to as Jesus) had returned with another request.

I had successfully completed Yeshua's request to write my first book, *Messiah Within – A Guide to Embracing Your Inner Divinity.* In this second request, He was asking me to expand beyond my role as spiritual author into the role of spiritual teacher.

It was not enough to just *talk the talk* of Spirituality as an author. Yeshua was asking me to *walk the walk* of Spirituality as a teacher. To move from *talking to walking* required me to align my day-to-day life with my spiritual life. It was from this place of alignment that I unlocked the 18 Keys to living a life that is connected and guided by the Divine.

To live a divinely guided life, I must live my *daily* life from the perspective of a spiritual being - and so must you. The 18 Keys provide divinely inspired teachings which support us on our spiritual journeys. Ultimately, by honoring these 18 Keys, we can embrace our connection to all beings and realize a deep state of Oneness.

As you may recall from *Messiah Within,* "The concept of Oneness begins as an intellectual exercise. We might read about it in a book such as this. But only as we begin to discover our own inner divinity can we recognize Oneness as an experience, not just a concept. It becomes part of who we are - at the core- and this is the ultimate gift from the Divine."

Yeshua, and many other Spiritual Masters, say that this profound shift from the experience of separation to Oneness is our purpose of this lifetime. To assist you in contemplating each of the 18 Keys, I have included a beautiful photograph of Mother Nature along with the text.

May the wisdom and beauty presented here guide you to *walk the walk* of Oneness throughout your life.

~ Robin H. Clare

The 18 Divine Keys consist of the following three sets of six Keys each:

- The first 6 Keys will help you access the Divine - anytime and anywhere - so you can come to understand the spiritual principles and *talk the talk.*
- The second set of 6 Keys will teach you how to tune-in to daily messages from the Divine - so you can *walk the talk* of spiritual principles in a more tangible and consistent way.
- The third set of 6 Keys will teach you how to live in harmony with the Divine every moment of every day - so you can faithfully *walk the walk* as a spiritual being having a human experience.

Important Tips for Embracing the 18 Divine Keys

Each of the 18 Divine Keys includes a contemplative question for you to consider. Please note that however you respond *will be perfect.* As you grow on your spiritual journey, your answers likely will change according to your deeper awareness - but for now, relax and enjoy the journey. To help you accomplish this, the following process is highly recommended:

1. Sit in a location that brings you serenity. Be sure to have a pencil or pen and paper or a special journal nearby.
2. Turn off all electronic communication devices.
3. Close your eyes and take a few deep breaths to center yourself.
4. Ask aloud for your Divine Source to be present with you during your contemplation of the Key.
5. Ask silently your Divine Source to help you quiet your mind and open your heart center.
6. Open your eyes and read the wisdom of the Key that you are focusing on.
7. Gaze at the photograph on the page while contemplating the message of the Key.
8. Focus on your heart center and ask, *what is the meaning of this Key's question in my life?*
9. As you continue to focus on your heart center, ask, *how can I integrate this Key into my daily life?*
10. Visualize yourself *actively living* this Key in a successful way.
11. Either silently or aloud, express deep gratitude for the support of your Divine Source.
12. Take a few minutes to write down the answer to the question asked or any spiritual guidance you received.

The 18 Divine Keys

Part 1

Talk the Talk

Dawn Breaks

The 1st Key

Discover Your Spiritual Identity

The spiritual journey begins on the inside and expands into the world you see. It officially begins when you declare your intention as: "I am a spiritual being having a human being experience."

At your deepest point of stillness, you begin to hear your inner voice whispering, "I Am One with All." Please know that this Loving Presence has always been a part of your life - you just may not have been aware of It before now.

Throughout this book, this Presence will be called the Divine. To know the Divine more deeply, step into your spiritual journey with a sense of curiosity, awe and desire.

You are beginning to actively seek out information that resonates with your new inner experience. Life becomes exciting and interesting as you awaken to the most profound truths of your life.

How would you define your spiritual identity?

The Gathering Begins

The 2nd Key

Meet Your Spiritual Support Team

Now that you have committed to your spiritual journey, it is important to know that you are not alone. In fact, you have such a big "team" accompanying you that once you feel their presence you may never feel alone again.

Your Spiritual Support Team are manifestations of the Divine. Your team is comprised of Spiritual Masters, angels, spirit guides, deceased loved ones and earth angels (which includes family, friends, coaches and teachers).

Each member of your Spiritual Support Team plays a unique role in your life. As you begin to acknowledge them, you will become aware of all the help that they can provide to you.

Your non-earthly Spiritual Support Team will not intervene unless you ask for help. Once you receive the help, you have free will to either follow or not follow the guidance.

Included in the upcoming keys are tools to help you connect with and fully utilize your unique Spiritual Support Team.

Who would you most like to connect with on your Spiritual Support Team?

The Pieces Await Retrieval

The 3rd Key

Heal Your Heart

A key aspect of the spiritual journey is to bring your heart back into a state of emotional and energetic wholeness.

Yeshua has shared that every person on the planet experiences a broken heart in one way or another. This can happen in many ways from an unrequited love to the loss of a loved one.

When your heart gets broken, you begin to love by *giving* pieces of your heart away; however, this *way* of loving does not truly serve yourself or others. The best way to serve yourself or others is to *retrieve* all of the pieces of your broken or shattered heart.

Only when you have retrieved all of the pieces of your heart, can it become healed and whole. From a healed heart you will be free to love more deeply and unconditionally.

Included at the end of the book is a Heart's Temple Ceremony, intended by the Ascended Masters to heal a broken or shattered heart.

Are you ready to heal your broken or shattered heart?

Prepare Your Temple

The 4th Key

Optimize Your Health and Well-Being

Imagine if the Divine was coming to your home (your Temple) and it was a mess. It is true that the Divine lives inside you and it is true that your body is your Temple. Do you maintain it as a dwelling worthy of a Divine Presence?

Your inner voice or intuition is your own private connection to the Divine. What you eat, the purity of the water you drink, and how well you breathe... these factors affect your brain and heart, which determines how well you can hear and heed the Divine' guidance.

When you are healthy there is more joy, peace, love and light shining in your Temple. This creates the ideal scenario for establishing greater spiritual connection.

It is also necessary to replace destructive patterns and self-limiting beliefs with ones that empower you to stay positive. Connecting with members of your earthly Spiritual Support Team can provide the support needed to become physically *and* spiritually fit!

How do you welcome the Divine into your Temple?

Rejoining the Flock

The 5th Key

Awaken into Oneness

You came from Oneness and you will return to Oneness. However, it has become part of the human experience to feel separated. When you feel the Divine presence inside of you, you begin to move from a feeling of separation into Oneness.

This is the essence of the spiritual experience on Earth: the journey back to knowing and feeling that you are One with all inhabitants on Earth and beyond.

To feel Oneness, you must be very present. This means being focused on what is happening in this exact moment in time, not regretting what has happened in the past, nor worrying about what might happen in the future.

These moments of presence and stillness bring you into the realization that you are One with All Being. It is an extraordinary gift to connect to the collective energies of all beings (both seen and unseen) known as All Being.

When do you notice the symmetry and peacefulness between all beings on our beautiful planet Earth?

On Your Journey

The 6th Key

Access the Wisdom of Your Heart

This key requires that you have completed the Heart's Temple Ceremony at the back of the book and that you are finding ways to be more present in your life. It is now time to access the wisdom of your healed heart.

We are trained to make decisions using only the logical aspects of the mind. Yet, a decision made from the healed heart is twice as powerful for realizing the highest and best outcomes for all.

Focusing on your healed heart for answers opens you to guidance from your Spiritual Support Team. By its very definition, the Universe has unlimited resources to help you!

To access the wisdom of your healed heart, you must quiet your mind. Only from this place of quiet stillness will the highest answers to your most pressing questions come into your awareness.

What situations in your life could benefit from a heart-centered perspective?

Part 2

Walk the Talk

Steadfast

The 7th Key

Become Committed

To truly master anything in life, you must first make a commitment to practicing a process. Commitment on the spiritual journey requires that you practice a process that is aligned with the Laws of the Universe.
The Law of Attraction is a Universal Law that explains how you can manifest anything in your life. Using this simple model for manifesting abundance can make it easier to become committed.

The Law of Attraction Model:

1. Set your intention.
2. Take right action to achieve your goal.
3. Release yourself from struggle by remembering this truth...

"When you believe it, you will see it." Dr. Wayne Dyer

How do you demonstrate commitment to your spiritual journey?

Emerge

The 8th Key

Recognize the Signs

The Divine speaks to you in a myriad of ways: a verbal message, a feeling, a sign, a gut instinct, goose bumps, synchronistic events or the arrival of help when you most need it.

The most exciting part is that the more you recognize and acknowledge the signs, the more they seem to occur and the more you notice them.

In actuality, the signs are always present - but you must be in a present-moment mindset in order to recognize them.

When you acknowledge the *extraordinary* happenings in your life, they happen more often and soon become your *normal* way of life.

What signs from the Divine are present in your day to day life?

The Gentle Flow of the Tide

The 9th Key

Stop and Listen

The Divine Guidance that is readily available will eventually become a natural part of your moment-to-moment life experience.

To reach this Divine way of living, you must learn to distinguish between what is the Voice of the Divine and what is the everyday noise of life.

Ways to quiet the mind include; meditation, prayer, walking, observing nature, gardening, even washing dishes! The choices are many, and how you quiet your mind is up to you.

The best way to still your emotions is to ask yourself whether you are looking at each situation from a perspective of love . . . or fear. It is the perspective of unconditional love that is the perspective of the Divine.

Ultimately, as you become more divinely guided, you will not have to STOP and listen, for you will be in the flow . . . and always hearing.

How will you place your busy life on pause
to hear the voice of the Divine?

Equilibrium

The 10th Key

Trust the Guidance

In Key 9, you learned how to stop and listen to the guidance available from the Divine. The challenge now is to *trust* what you are hearing.

Are you hearing your ego's logical solution that protects you from harm? Or are you hearing your heart's divinely guided solution?

The answer is both!

Logic and caution are often warranted, but prioritizing the Universal perspective of the Divine will help you make more impactful and beneficial choices for your life.

You are invited to *think from your heart* when making any life decision. When you think from your heart, your decisions will be made with greater compassion for yourself and others.

Where in your life do you find the balance between your mind and heart?

Universal Beauty

The 11th Key

Express Gratitude

Expressing gratitude is a master key for a divinely guided person - it unlocks many doors. Gratitude is a simple and direct means for becoming, and staying, deeply connected with the Divine.

From the moment of awakening, throughout the day, and before going to bed, expressing gratitude is therefore paramount.

Beyond your simple "thank you" for all of your blessings, there are many ways to express gratitude. Being of service to others is a very powerful expression of gratitude. Staying positive and greeting others with a beautiful smile... both are wonderful ways to express your gratitude.

The more gratitude you express, the more the world expands to share abundance with you.

How can you create a practice of gratitude in your life?

GO Fishing!

The 12th Key

Take Action

Set your intention for what you most desire, listen for guidance and then take action. Your taking action informs the Divine that you are very serious about creating what you intend.

Even one small step forward will set the proper energy in motion for you to reach your desired state of abundance. The Divine will encourage you to continue moving forward by lighting your path with inspiring ideas and synchronistic events.

The Divine will also let you know when a course correction may be warranted along the way. Sometimes a course correction can at first feel like frustration and disappointment.

Remember, there are no mistakes, only opportunities for course corrections!

What is the next step required for achieving your most pressing goal?

Part 3

Walk the Walk

Sacred Beauty

The 13th Key

Create Sacred Space

"*Come, sit and listen.*" whispers the Divine.

The Divine speaks quietly, using words, signs and physical sensations, such as goose bumps.

The best place to hear the Divine is in a setting where you feel peaceful, present and quiet.

This deep listening can occur in a meditation space in your home, at a beautiful location in nature, or at a gathering of like-minded community.

By creating sacred space in your life, you are inviting the Divine into your life with a very clear message that says, *"I am ready to listen."*

Where is your sacred space?

Stand in Your Power

The 14th Key

Have Faith in Your Beliefs

Deep in your heart, you are very clear about your beliefs. You have carried forth your beliefs or standards derived from past experiences and the influence of important people in your life.

These beliefs and standards have helped to define the person you are today. Yet, every moment of every day, other people in the world are constantly shouting their beliefs at you. It's no wonder that confusion is a natural state of mind.

You are encouraged to have faith in your beliefs and you are invited to expand your beliefs to include deeper and richer spiritual teachings. This expanded perspective will enable you to take pride in your personal beliefs while being more tolerant of others' beliefs.

What are your personal beliefs?

Reflection

The 15th Key

Ground the Divine in You

Many of us were taught to meditate, or pray, by going to an imaginary place. This place is outside of our physical vessel, and often feels beyond our reach, especially when we need it most.

True connection to the Divine requires that you find this spiritual place within your own Temple... within your Inner Divinity.

Bring *Heaven to Earth* in your meditation, by focusing on your own heart center. Focus on feeling the loving energy inside your own body, rather than in an imaginary place.

When your vessel is filled with this loving energy, all the love, peace and joy that you gathered internally will shine out into the world you see.

How can you bring Heaven to Earth in your meditation or prayer practice?

Stopping the Churn

The 16th Key

Live AS Love

At this stage of your spiritual journey, you have had many opportunities to experience the love and light of the Divine.

The ultimate experience is to *live as love* in all aspects of life.

This means that you no longer allow destructive, fear-based emotions to hijack your attention and steal your Divine energy.

Processing - and then *letting go* - of worry, guilt, hatred and revenge will make space for the miraculous healing power of love to guide your life.

"You'll find, as you look back upon your life, that the
moments when you have truly lived are the moments
when you have done things in the spirit of love."
- Author Unknown

What negative emotions do you need to let go of today to live as love?

Clearing Skies

The 17th Key

Integrate Mind, Body, Spirit and Emotion

Being a human being is complicated. Each one of us is comprised of four components: mind, body, spirit and emotion. Any event that impacts one of the components has an indirect effect on all the other components.

This level of inter-connectedness creates a need to integrate all of the components into one highly functioning, synergistic being. This can occur by implementing a healing and growth plan that emphasizes all four components.

As a fully-integrated and highly functioning being, you align your human being with your spiritual being. From this place, you will learn to love all aspects of yourself in an unconditional manner.

When you fill yourself with unconditional love, what overflows from you will always include enough for others.

How can you express unconditional love for yourself?

Harmony

The 18th Key

Become One with the Divine

By embracing *The Divine Keys*, you have opened your awareness to this sacred truth, *You Are One with the Divine.* The biggest challenge is remembering that this is true, especially when life distracts you with so many ways to feel separate from the Divine.

Say aloud: "I am One with the Divine." Notice what you feel in your body and hear in your mind when you say this aloud. If there is discomfort or disagreement, please return to page 1 and start this process over.

The more you repeat this process, the more you will calmly experience the knowing that the Divine is just a breath away for guidance and company.

Live your divinely guided life with the confidence that the Divine is delighted to share your life with you … seeing the world through your extraordinary eyes.

How will you share your life with the Divine?

The Heart's Temple Ceremony™ for retrieving and mending your broken or shattered heart

Step #1 - Make a list of the most significant people or pets that you have shared a piece of your heart with (i.e. those people that you have loved). The people or pets can be alive or deceased. Please note that it does not matter whether they have hurt you or not, it just matters that you loved them.
Step #2 – Every person or pet has an energetic signature. For each person or pet, you will recall that when you think of him/her, you have a different sensation in your heart. This is their energetic signature resonating with you.
Step #3 - As you call in a person or pet from the list, it is very important that you share forgiveness with him/her and imagine that he/she shares forgiveness with you for any hurts that you may have bestowed upon each other.
Step #4 - When you are complete with the forgiveness process, visualize him/her placing the piece of your energetic heart back into your hands to place back into your energetic chest.
Step #5 - With the heart piece placed back in, imagine that you have a golden thread and needle and you are sewing the piece back into your energetic heart.
Step #6 - When you have completed the sewing of the pieces back into your heart, take the time to journal about the experience with each of the loved ones.

Note: Please do not hesitate to take back a piece of your heart from someone that you truly love today. This ceremony is intended to help you to love this person or pet from a whole heart and not just by the piece of your heart that you shared with them.

About Robin H. Clare

Robin has 25 years of experience as a seasoned corporate MBA and now supports spiritual seekers full time for more than a decade. Robin serves as a channel for the Ascended Masters, an advanced Akashic Record reader and as a highly regarded spiritual teacher. She is the author of *Messiah Within*, *The Divine Keys* and an upcoming book entitled *Being of Service*. Robin is honored to live her life's purpose in service to others. To learn more about Robin, please go to www.clare-ity.com.

About Garrett Clare

Garrett is a full-time student at the University of Maine where he studies New Media. His deep appreciation for Mother Nature is clearly illustrated by the photos in this book, which would not be complete without his artistic heart. After living in Brooklyn, New York for two summers, Garrett has also developed an extensive portfolio of high-impact concert photography. To see more of Garrett's photography, please go to: www.garrettclare.format.com.

Made in the USA
San Bernardino, CA
24 January 2018